AIM

TANNI GREY THOMPSON

ACCENT PRESS LTD

Published by Accent Press Ltd – 2007
ISBN 1905170890/9781905170890
Copyright © Tanni Grey Thompson 2007

The Quick Reads project in Wales is a joint venture between the Basic
Skills Agency and the Welsh Books Council. Titles are funded through
the Basic Skills Agency as part of the National Basic Skills Strategy for
Wales on behalf of the Welsh Assembly Government.

Printed and bound in the UK

Cover Design by Emma Barnes

INTRODUCTION

I'm glad to be able to share my experiences with you and I sincerely hope that they will be useful in helping you to Aim High, in your own life.

Aiming High has been one of my own personal mottos throughout not only my sporting life, but my personal life as well. In simple terms it is all about trying to be the best that you can.

This book is divided into two parts, firstly my early life, how I got started in sport, and what inspired me (and still inspires me!). Secondly how my sporting life has developed, the secrets behind my success and the lessons I have learned along the way. If these lessons help you, this book will have achieved its purpose.

Sport is one of the biggest loves of my life, but I am also passionate about reading – my husband laughs at me because I really will read anything! I hope you enjoy reading *Aim High*. It was a challenge to work on it, but one of my beliefs, linked to Aiming High, is that if you don't try you never know what you can do... finishing this book is proof of that!

PART ONE
CHAPTER ONE

Growing Up

We have a picture in our family album of me sitting in my first little red wheelchair wearing a Brownie uniform, with little knobbly knees and wearing some dodgy trainers. The picture was taken not long after I started using a wheelchair and we were on a Brownie 'pack holiday' in Swansea.

The strange thing about this picture is that I am trying to skip. It looks funny, as all the other Brownies are behind me (all non-disabled), skipping away with different levels of ability.

The reason that this picture is really important to me is that it shows that no one ever told me that I shouldn't skip, and no one ever told me that I shouldn't try. It confirms that, as I was growing up, my parents never told me there were things I couldn't do solely because I was a wheelchair user. There were plenty of times that I was told off for doing something (possibly naughty), but I was never told off simply for trying.

If my parents had been different, if they had had low expectations for me, I could have grown up thinking very differently. But for me it was about having the chance to try, and seeing what I might achieve. If someone had told me that I couldn't skip I might have found this out a little sooner than I did, but then I might have spent the next five years thinking 'what if'. My parents were both only children, and had quite restricted upbringings, and I think this is part of the reason why they always encouraged us to go out and try things.

The reason that I became a wheelchair user has never been particularly important to me. I was born with a condition called Spina Bifida, and to begin with my disablement wasn't obvious. I had a tiny lump on my back. After spending a short time in an incubator I was sent home and everything seemed OK. My elder sister Sian, who is eighteen months older than me, hadn't had an easy time of it. She was born with a heart condition that was fixed with some fairly major surgery (these days it is through a key-hole procedure near the groin). It was then found that she had been born with dislocated hips, which resulted in eighteen months in a frog plaster, and after only a couple of days out of that, she fell and broke her leg. My parents certainly had their hands full for a couple of years!

I could walk till about the age of five or six (I don't remember exactly). But as I grew, my legs couldn't support the increase in my body weight, because of my condition, and I slowly became paralysed. So I didn't, unlike others, have to suffer some dramatic accident, or spend months on end in a spinal unit. For me, becoming a wheelchair user wasn't an awful experience. Although I had stopped walking I didn't feel that something had been taken away. Having said this, the last few months when I *was* walking were pretty tough – this was the only time in my life that I have felt really disabled. I couldn't do the things that I wanted to do – like run away from my mum!

Having a wheelchair gave me a renewed sense of freedom. Because many people think that the life of a wheelchair user is pretty miserable, they make judgements about it. But the wheelchair allowed me once again to do the things that I wanted to do, such as trying to run away from my mother, chasing after my older sister, and being with my friends.

I was born on 26th July 1969, and had the good fortune to be born in Cardiff, the capital of Wales. My sister Sian and I were brought up in the house my dad grew up in. Mum is also a Cardiff girl and Cardiff, a great city, is very much my home town. I'm very proud of being Welsh and that I've been voted Welsh Sports Personality of the Year on three occasions.

Dad is an architect; he's a very organized person, who likes to know what he is doing and when. I hope some of this has rubbed off on me, but in temperament I'm more like Mum – if we decide that we want to do something, then we want to do it right now! I have a tendency to think quickly about what I want to do, sometimes making rash decisions as a result.

Sian was a great sister to grow up with; she wasn't that interested in taking part in sport when she was young, although she watched a lot, and has always been incredibly supportive, often travelling with me to events and helping to pay for stuff (as did my parents).

She's not as competitive as me, but then very few people are! I always knew that I wanted to do sport, and that I had to compete as hard as I could.

Unfortunately, I didn't really get to know my grandparents, also all from Cardiff, who died before I was old enough to remember them well. My dad's father was a very good motorbike rider, who competed in the TT races. He was unable to turn professional, though, and had to get a real job.

My primary school was really inclusive in terms of letting me take part in PE lessons. It was different in secondary school because the rules were different. There were a number of disabled children in the school and it was felt that we should do our PE at the special school next door. It wasn't that I didn't really want to go to the special school, but I didn't know anyone there. I had some good PE teachers who let me join in with my friends as much as possible.

To be honest, I didn't really know what Spina Bifida was until I was about ten years old. I didn't actively try to find out because it didn't matter to me what had stopped me walking. I just knew that I couldn't walk, and that there was nothing I could do to change that, so I just had to get on with it. This wasn't a conscious decision. There were simply lots of things that I wanted to do, and I wanted to spend my time doing them, not sitting around thinking about what I *couldn't* do.

Many people who become wheelchair users don't feel this way, and I know that some of them find my attitude challenging. For many young people, a tragic accident – which is sometimes their fault, sometimes someone else's – means that they can no longer do things the way that they used to. For them, it means learning everything again from scratch, from dressing themselves to driving. But my rehab all took place while I was slowly losing the use of my legs, so it never really felt like 'rehab'. It felt normal.

Spina Bifida isn't anyone's fault, although over the years I have learnt that it can have many causes – previous family illnesses, poor diet, living near coal mines, for instance. These days it is accepted that folic acid does make a difference (and lack of it could have caused my condition), so every pregnant women or a woman thinking of having a baby is advised to take it. But the cause never really bothered me. It could have been the man on the moon who caused my impairment, and this would certainly have made a more exciting story! Some people find it hard to believe that I have honestly never spent any time thinking about what I didn't have. But the last couple of years when I was trying to walk were hard, and I don't really remember a time when walking was easy. So I didn't have a great deal to compare my situation with. All I knew at the time was that occasionally I had to go for hospital checkups, where I was prodded and poked around, and then I came home.

My parents had a lot more to cope with than I did, because they had more idea what was going on. They had to make decisions about my mobility, what treatment I would or wouldn't have, and they had more knowledge than I did about what my long-term expectations might be. In fact, they kept me blissfully unaware of these expectations until I was in my thirties.

But if I was unconcerned about my impairment, how did – or do – other people deal with it?

My mother always said that she had too many things to worry about and that she didn't have time to feel sorry for anyone, let alone herself – life was just too busy.

Some people, however, seem to think that wheelchair users are somehow different from ordinary people, and that we don't deserve privacy in the same way. These people think they have an automatic right to ask wheelchair users any question they like. If I had a pound for every person who has stopped me in the street and said 'So, what's wrong with you, then?' I would be a rich woman! Another favourite is, 'So, are you confined to your wheelchair, then', to which I have replied, 'Yes, I usually sleep in it!' My humour is not always appreciated. But what most people want to know is how I came to be a wheelchair user. Most tend to assume that something a lot more dramatic than a congenital birth defect must have caused it. It almost feels as if they would like the cause to be something more romantic.

Some of these people are just plain nosey, but there are others who seem to think that a disabled person doesn't have any feelings, and is obliged to answer questions from complete strangers. These encounters have never made me feel particularly uncomfortable, but I haven't always answered the questions.

If I had had a different upbringing – if I had not had positive people around me, not fought to go into mainstream school – I don't think I would have been able to deal with my situation so well.

If people have low expectations for disabled people – in fact, if they have low expectations for *any* young people – this has an effect on what the young people are able to do later on in life. Some youngsters manage to rise above it, but too many young people with disabilities grow up believing that they cannot achieve, because the people around them don't believe it.

I remember at school one careers teacher told me that I should go to secretarial college and learn to type, because people in wheelchairs became receptionists! I didn't listen to that – when I told him that I wanted to go to university he told me that I was probably wasting my time as it wouldn't help me get a job!

If there was one thing that I could change, then it would be for young disabled people to naturally assume that they have a right to do everything their non-disabled counterparts are doing. Not, as is so often the case now, to assume that there is a whole pile of things that they will never do.

In the UK we like to attach labels to people, and more often than not we define and judge people by the job that they do, or the level they reach within that job. Because of this, disabled people lose out. Many people look at impairment and the first thing they think of is what *cannot* be achieved. If we consider that a person with a disability has no status, because they are limited in what they can do, this can set the tone for the relationship.

As an athlete I have spent the best part of the last twenty years trying to be the best that I can. Being an athlete has been what I have wanted to do for almost as long as I can remember, but there are many other labels that people could attach to me. I could be a mother, an athlete, a woman, a graduate – many things. But there was one thing that I was sure about when I was growing up – I didn't want to be labelled as disabled.

CHAPTER TWO

Getting Started in Sport

Competing for Britain had always been my ambition but, in the early years, I actually wanted to play basketball. I didn't think athletics was very exciting. It didn't help that disability sport had a very limited profile in the mid-1980s. To my mind there were two people, both Welsh, who did an incredible amount of work to change this. They were John Harris and Chris Hallam, and they were something of a double act. Chris came across as brash, while John was quietly humorous. I remember watching a documentary on them and their sporting careers (I was only just embarking on mine) and John was asked what he missed most now that he was in a wheelchair. He looked towards the camera and smiled, and said that it was his mam warming his socks in the oven in the morning. When asked what he would most like to do, he said 'have a heart attack running for a bus'. There was no self-pity, only a little self-mockery, and I thought that this was a cool way to handle being in a wheelchair. Meanwhile Chris, from Cwmbran, with his bleached-blond hair, and tiger-print racing suits, was competing in, and winning, the London marathon, where I saw him race in 1985. Between them they stirred up the world of disability sport!

I knew after playing just a few games of basketball that it wasn't for me. There weren't many teams around, which made training hard, and I knew that I didn't want to play only every couple of months. I wanted much more than that. Then I played at a junior basketball weekend at Stoke Mandeville, and there was an unfortunate incident on the court where I slapped someone! I knew I had to look for something else. If I couldn't control my temper, it wasn't the right thing for me.

From the moment I started doing athletics, I knew I'd found my sport. My first race was at about the age of 12 and I knew from the first moment I did it that this was what I wanted to do. It wasn't easy to find somewhere to train, but I persisted. It took a couple of years to find a coach and a club, and longer to find the right way to train, but I think the early difficulties taught me a lot about how, if you really want something, you have to work at it.

I needed a lot of support from my family too, because of the places that they had to take me to train, and because of the time that I was away from home.

Some people have stacks of natural talent, and from the outside it can seem as if everything just appears to work out for them. This can feel a little unfair – you are slogging your way through mundane tasks while they appear to float through to achievement without a care in the world.

But the saying 'appearances can be deceptive' is true. Usually we can't see the grind that people go through. We don't see what is happening in their personal life, and people rarely admit that things are harder than they appear. We all like to make out that achievement is 'easy', and that everything has happened exactly as we planned it.

I have worked with different coaches over the years. The relationship between a coach and an athlete is a unique thing. Finding the right person to work with is not always easy, as the coach has to be a cross between a mentor, mother, chief whip, guidance counsellor and numerous other things! They also have to have experience of the sport, and have great communication skills.

I have worked with four coaches so far (if you count my husband Ian) and I have also spent a fair chunk of my athletic career being self-coached. In the early years this was because there weren't too many people volunteering to coach wheelchair racers, and, in the latter years, it was because I liked having control over my own destiny.

The first coach I worked with was Roy Anthony; he was based with Bridgend Athletics Club in south Wales. He worked with me in my early years, before I went to university. He had a great sense of humour, understood the group mentality of teenage girls, and could get the best out of most people that he worked with. When winter training was hard, he would use a mixture of encouragement and cajoling, and sessions were always fun. I used to love some of the winter sessions when we would be sprinting up and down the local multi-storey car park. Of course, in this day and age, child protection and health and safety regulations wouldn't let us do that, but we had a terrific time. Everyone I knew who worked with Roy gave him 110% because that was what he expected and we wanted to show him that we could do it.

As I developed as an athlete (and moved further away from home), I found that I enjoyed playing a bigger part in what I was doing. I enjoyed writing training programmes and working out what I needed to do. I also enjoyed learning about how the sport worked, the real practicalities of who did what, within the team. I always wanted to understand how the system worked, because I knew that understanding this was important if you were ambitious (which I was). I needed to know not only what it would take in performance terms to qualify (i.e. what times I had to achieve), but also what other skills I needed to be selected.

I learnt never to be afraid to ask questions. I have learnt so much from other athletes. Many of the best athletes in the world – such as Jeff Adams from Canada, and Heinz Frei from Switzerland – were happy to share information about how they had achieved what they had. I always thought that this was amazingly generous, and also kind. They didn't need to spend time doing it, but they did, because they were confident in their own ability and they cared about the development of the sport.

I learnt that if someone is successful it is important to look at what they are doing and how they are doing it, and learn from it, but not to copy it exactly. Training programmes, for example, set for one person, cannot always be followed by another. You have to take into account everything else the athlete has done to get to the point they are at. One young athlete I knew talked to a much older experienced athlete about the training sessions they did. These were about four times as strenuous as the young athlete was doing, and because the older athlete had been successful, the younger one started to mirror the sessions. There was a big jump in improvement in the short term, but after a few months the younger athlete started to suffer. He became tired, and picked up a few injuries. Because he wasn't used to the training load, and hadn't built it up gradually, his body couldn't cope. It resulted in injury and a long lay-off from the sport. So the moral is: always learn from other people, but then adapt and improve on it.

Two of the other coaches that I've worked with in my career are Dave Williams and Jenni Banks. They acted in very different capacities.

Dave Williams worked through Cardiff Athletics Club. I joined the club when I graduated from Loughborough University and he acted as a training advisor for a number of years. He had never coached a wheelchair athlete before we worked together, but his help with planning saw me in good stead for many years.

Then, after a number of years coaching myself, I decided that I needed to hand over some of that responsibility to someone else for a while. I was finding that there was more pressure on my time due to work commitments and training, and I was enjoying less and less the planning and writing of programmes.

Jenni Banks is Australian and in the early 1990s was working with some of the best athletes in the world. She had taken them from being young and developmental and helped them become world beaters. This was part of the reason that I chose her, but it was also because she listened. She listened to what I said I wanted to achieve, and she would tell me straight if she thought I wasn't pulling my weight. That honesty was sometimes hard to hear, but it made me a better athlete. She helped me structure not only my athletics life, but also my personal life too.

Jenni had been a hockey player, and an injury early on in her career had stopped her reaching her goal of playing for the Australian Olympic team. The transition had been tough for her. She had been through an emotional and traumatic time. Her dream had been ripped away from her. One of the most valuable things she taught me was that while wheelchair racing was important, life was important too. You always had to have other things in your life. Not things that would distract you from competing, but that could complement it. Things that would help in life after sport. Very few people make enough money from sport not to have to work again. And most people want to do something with their lives after sport, whether they need the money or not.

Jenni helped me think about working, about putting something back into sport. I have always been keen to understand how the business of sport worked, and the time I spent with Jenni made me think about playing a role in sports administration. She pointed out that if I cared about my sport, then I should also care about what happened to it. (Though sometimes, these days, I think I care too much, and that there are some things that I should just step away from!)

As I get older my physio and my masseur become more and more important. I remember visiting my physio one day and telling her that when I held my arm at a particular angle and moved it up and down, it hurt. She looked at me, and asked two questions. She asked whether I needed to do that for daily life. I said no. She then asked me if I needed to use that action for anything to do with training or competing. Again I said no. She looked at me for a moment, and then told me she had the answer to my discomfort. She told me to just stop moving it that way!

At my stage of an athletics career, injury is part of the deal. You have to minimize it, but you can sometimes over-analyse and worry about things that aren't significant. I still monitor what my body can do. I check that problems I have now aren't getting worse, because they could affect me later on in life. But if they aren't, I leave them alone.

I'm glad to have the chance to publicly acknowledge and thank these people who have been so important to me, and whose contributions have been so significant. When I hear sportspeople saying that they have achieved things on their own I laugh – this is rarely true.

CHAPTER THREE

Aim High – Motivation and Inspiration

'Aim High' is part of a saying that my grandfather taught my mother, and she in turn taught me. The full saying is a bit daft, and doesn't mean a lot until you explain it fully, but it has kept me going throughout my athletics career and personal life. It is 'Aim high, even if you hit a cabbage'. In essence it is about having a goal and a dream, and seeing what you can achieve. If you don't try, you will never do anything. In today's world we seem obsessed with non-achievement, and seem to want to protect every young person from the difficulties that failure brings. I can honestly say that in all the years that I have been competing there are only a few races that I have 'failed' at. There are plenty of races that I haven't won, but that to me is something completely different.

You need to be on the start line to have a chance of winning. You cannot win a medal if the furthest step you have taken is going to a few training sessions or sitting in the stands. To me, the worst type of failure is someone saying, 'I could have been...' You can add any ending you like to the rest of the sentence. I knew lots of talented young people in school, but not all got up off their backsides and did something to capitalise on it. And then there are lots of athletes who train hard – but what you also have to do is train smart, and this is not the same thing.

Many businesses have mottos, or mission statements. In my case I had my motto before I had my 'business', and before I really understood what it meant, but as I grew up in my sport, and developed a sense of what I was trying to achieve, I realised that it was the best motto that I could possibly have.

I write 'Aim high, even if you hit a cabbage' in the front of every one of my training diaries. It is the first page that I see when I open it, and it is there to inspire me in everything I do. I no longer need to write it down anywhere else, because it is with me all the time, but every time I write it in a new book it re-affirms what I think about the way I train.

In fact, the way that I plan my athletics life is little different from how people plan their business lives. I always compare my training plan to a personal development plan. And my end-of-season analysis is a bit like a business personal review, with my head coach, who is in effect my boss.

The difference is that we are measured not by how many reports we write, whether we hit our sales targets or not, or even by the input of our training, but by the medals that we win at major Games. There are lesser targets – I might work on a particular weakness in the way that I handle my chair, or design new gloves that will help me climb hills better – but there are major Games almost every year, culminating in the Paralympics every four years, and this is where we really have to deliver. So our 'personal review' is, unfortunately, more public than many others!

And the public can be harsh critics. If they think I haven't done a good enough job there are plenty who will stop me in the street and tell me!

Success can mean a lot of different things. In wheelchair racing it is about winning medals. But there is no guarantee of success and sometimes you can have the best race of your life and come sixth. Sometimes you can perform averagely and win! And there is every combination in between. It is important to learn to differentiate between bad winning and good losing.

The media might not understand how coming sixth can be a good performance, the team might not, but what is important is that you and your coach understand what your performance means at all times. This is one way of learning about what you have done, and moving on for the future.

Some people think I have an obsession with athletics, though I like to think that I am merely 'focused'. I don't really remember when my interesting sport went from being just fun, to serious work. It happened a long time ago. But I haven't felt any loss, because the fun element has never disappeared.

The fact is, though, that just about every major decision in my life has been affected by me being a competitor: from the man who I married, and when the wedding would be, to where we went on honeymoon, to the timing of having our daughter.

I believe that if you are serious about something, you need to treat it seriously. And I haven't had to sacrifice anything on the way – truthfully, all my decisions have been what I have wanted to do.

But of course I do have a personal life, and I try hard to balance my family and racing career. I look at newspaper stories about women who work in the City, get paid a squillion pounds a year, yet have lots of kids, go to yoga, make organic yoghurt and still have time to get their eyebrows waxed. I feel a kind of awe. Most of the time in our house, I feel that we just about get by.

I went through a brief phase where I felt I wasn't being a good enough mother because I wasn't doing all of the above. But the guilt didn't last long. I realised that being a good mother wasn't all about mashing carrots that I had grown myself – there were plenty of reputable companies out there mashing up baby food for me! And does it matter if Carys very occasionally has crisps for breakfast? I don't think so. Just as I prioritize my working life, the same is true in my personal life.

There are no wholly right or wrong answers. We all have to compromise. But a good work-life balance is essential, and we need to work at it and not take it for granted.

Whatever you do in life, and whatever decisions you make, there may be a price to be paid. You have to decide at all points if that price is worth paying.

Lots of journalists have asked me what I have had to sacrifice in my life in order to do sport. But, for me, the answer is really easy. It is nothing. My family have given up a lot of things in order to allow me to be an athlete, but I have been privileged.

It has always been what I have wanted to do, more than anything else.

PART TWO
CHAPTER FOUR

My Sporting Life

When I am asked to try and describe what my life has been like as an athlete, it is hard to put it into words.

Throughout my wheelchair racing career, my goals have constantly changed. In the early years, when I was moving out of the junior ranks and into the senior group, my goals were just about making the national team. It was touch and go whether I would make Seoul, and I think that I only just scraped in. By the time I got to Barcelona in 1992 I had broken the world records for the four distances that I compete in, but still had people to beat. Atlanta was about not losing, and Sydney was about just being the best that I could be. Athens was a whole other event. I went through huge ups and downs in those Games which made me realise that, although wheelchair racing was really important to me, it wasn't everything in my life. More about that later.

Competing for the national team can be amazing. I still remember when my first selection letter came through for a major Games. I didn't know if I was going to make it into the team or not until I got the letter, and was so excited when I knew I was going to Seoul. This was in 1988.

Being a member of the national team was a dream come true. And indeed it is a wonderful, exhilarating experience. It is also challenging and sometimes scary, but I wouldn't change a moment of it.

One of the most successful events in my life as an athlete was competing in 1992 at the Barcelona Paralympics Games. I won a total of five medals – four gold and one silver – and became the first woman to break the one minute barrier in the 400 metres. For these Games there was a dramatic increase in the coverage of the Paralympic Games, and also a sea change in the way that the Games were covered. For the first time there was lots of mainstream coverage, and it was covered as sport, not as poor disabled people being brave and marvellous.

I remember returning home to the UK to meet my family, and, while watching some of the coverage on TV, my mother told me that I looked like someone she had previously seen on the telly. I reacted like any young woman would – I was flattered that she thought I looked like someone who was famous! My mum then told me that she thought I looked like the character called Olive from *On the Buses*! Olive was a lot older than I was, and about three times my body weight! But she had a similar bob and glasses to mine. I decided that this was Mum's way of telling me to get my hair cut! (In fact, throughout my career I have probably had far too many bad hairstyles, which at the time I always thought were trendy!)

My family has always been an integral part of what I have done, and helped me learn about my sport. Whatever I have done, and whatever I have achieved in my life, my family has always been there to support me.

Planning is so important. My experience at the Sydney Games illustrates this. There were people in the team who thought I should only enter three races and work really hard to win them. They didn't want me to try for four. But it was what I had been training for over a long period of time, and although it was hard, I persuaded them.

My first final was the 800 metres. I remember sitting on the warm-up track and feeling quite calm. But then, talking with a couple of the coaches, I started to feel nervous. I heard that the stadium was full. My sister was in the stadium – she had been there for several hours making sure that she got the best seats near the finish line. I got a message to her and told her what my race tactics were going to be. The plan was that I would sit in lane two on the edge of pack and wait for a sprint finish. I had used the same tactics a couple of times that year against the USA girls, and had done well. But once the gun went off, I changed my mind. I knew that I had a really strong finish and over the final 400 metres I could pull ahead and do well, but I decided that I would go to the front straight away, and pull the speed out of the pack. I was lucky, because indecision can be fatal. But, as it happened, it worked. I was so relieved. However, when I went to meet my sister after the race, the first thing she said was, 'you didn't race the way you told me'.

Winning the 800 metres gave me confidence, and the 100 metres was next, probably my weakest event at these Games. The main competitor to beat was an American athlete called Cheri Blauwet. She had been ill during the run up to the Games and had had a tough time competing, but was still a threat. However, I won, and after that – though there was a lot of pressure – the 200 metres went OK.

For the final of the 400 metres, I knew I had a chance of doing really well, but also knew that I had to push a really smart race. The night before the final we got the lane allocations and I found that I had drawn lane seven. I was number one in the world, was the world record holder and hadn't been beaten that season over 400 metres, but I was used to racing this distance in middle lanes. I would be unable to see where any of my fellow competitors were until the last 90 metres. I sat and talked it through with my husband Ian, but knew that there was only one way that I could race it – the same way that I raced every other race that season.

I split the 400 metres into four sections. I have a specific tactic for each section which I've always used whatever level I've competed at. So in the final I just did what I've always done and ran to the race plan that I'd worked on over the years. At about 250 metres into the race, I did take a very quick glance at the score board to see where my competitors were –

probably only about half a second behind – but I could sense that I was OK.

I did indeed win, and in a good time, and the point is that it was a good race. I stuck to the plan that I had worked on over the years, and it worked. I couldn't change the fact that I had drawn lane seven, but what I could do was race the way I knew how.

Everyone experiences challenges that get in the way of what we are trying to do. Sometimes these challenges are much larger than everyday problems, and they can grow until they seem almost too big to deal with.

They may seem as if they come from nowhere. Everything suddenly goes wrong. Or it could be a problem that has gradually built up over time, and then suddenly takes centre stage in our lives. However the problem occurs, it can cloud our ability to make sensible decisions. Sometimes our brains just seem to close down and we cannot see solutions.

However, solutions usually exist. They may not be what we would ideally like to do, and they may be daunting. But they are there. We have to learn to step back, and see them.

When I was training for the Atlanta Games

in 1996, I had many problems. It was a tough training year, and there were many other calls on my time. By the time I got to compete at the Games, I knew that it was going to be difficult for me to do well. I had qualified for the Olympic Games demonstration race, coming fourth overall, but the Paralympics were going to be different.

As it happens I raced well, broke several of my personal best records, and came away with one gold medal and three silvers. But there were members of the team who were disappointed, and felt that I had let them down. I hadn't won the four gold medals that I won in Barcelona. How the team is perceived is based on the number of gold medals won – that is how countries are compared with each other. Looking back now, I doubt I could have done better but, even so, it was hard for me, coming back from the Games, and having people tell me that they thought I had failed.

One of the options put to me was that I should retire. One of the team coaches even offered to write a press release for me, to announce it to the media. The temptation was there. At the time, it almost felt that this was the only choice open to me.

But my father had always told me that the best thing to do with a problem was to sleep on it, and I do believe that, if no instant decision needs to be taken, it is always worth taking time to consider one's options.

So I told the coaches that there was no need for me to make a decision there and then. I would wait and think about it when I got home, back to my home environment, with people I knew around me. Waiting was one of the best decisions I've ever made. By the time I got home I realised that retiring wasn't the right thing for me at all. I might not get selected again, I might never improve, but there was one thing I was sure of – I loved the sport of wheelchair racing. I still wanted to be the best I could be, and I could still do that, regardless of whether or not I was doing it in a GB vest. I carried on training for another eight years, and won six more Paralympic Gold medals.

Of course, to many of the general public I hadn't failed at all in Atlanta. My profile was high. I appeared on *Question of Sport*, and also *This is Your Life*. It was a strange experience, having my life run through in twenty-nine minutes, and it brought together a lot of my friends.

I must say I enjoy the way my sporting achievements have brought me into the public eye. Other highlights have been having my wedding featured in *Hello!* magazine and having the opportunity to appear on *The Weakest Link* and *Mastermind.*

It's partly, I suppose, because I enjoy the attention, but also it all helps to get across the message that I am keen to promote: that I want all young people to have the chance to participate in sport.

Over the years I have, of course, made some incorrect, or even bad, decisions. Probably more than I realise. But I also know that because the decisions I have taken have felt right at the time, I have rarely had regrets. There are some things I would do differently now, but I know you cannot go back. You have to learn from every decision, even if it is hard to admit your own failings, and keep moving forward.

Athens was a particularly difficult Games for me. I went into it as one of the most successful Paralympians of all time. I went in as British, European, World and Paralympic champion and record holder in a number of events. I qualified for the Olympic demonstration race in the 800 metres, but didn't compete well.

Going into the Paralympics, I did lots of media interviews where journalists asked me what I thought I could achieve. I believed I could win two golds, a silver and a bronze. This was based on what I had done in the past year, and the current form as I saw it of the athletes who were likely to be there.

I performed well in the semi-final. I did a decent time, and then got a good lane draw for the final. On the warm-up track I felt OK, and seemed to be preparing well, but then something happened. Going in to the final waiting area on the track, I just knew that I wasn't going to perform well that day. I had had these feelings before, though the other way around. A couple of times in my career I have suddenly known, just before the race, that without a shadow of a doubt I was going to go out there and break a world record, or win the race.

This was the first time that I sensed I could fail. And, of course, negative feelings do affect your destiny.

I started well, but was indecisive about what I was going to do – this was about 100 metres into the race. I didn't know whether to go to the front, or to try to sit in the pack and wait for a sprint finish. This indecisiveness not only cost me a medal (my prediction had been that I could win a silver), it cost me the chance of getting placed anywhere. I knew from 400 metres from the finish that I was going to come nowhere.

I had come to the Games a champion, and this was my worst position in a Paralympics race, probably my worst 800 metres ever, and the event was shown live on national TV. I felt that I had let a large number of people down – the people who had come to watch me race, my family, my team, and also myself.

I remember going to the side of the track, and I just started crying. By the time I got to where Ian was standing I could see he was visibly upset too – most unusual for him. I looked across to where the BBC camera crew was sitting, waiting for me to give an interview, and you could tell that they didn't really know what to do.

They gave me the option to do the interview later, but I believe in confronting demons. If I win I am more than happy to head over to the BBC and talk to them. They did an interview that asked some tough questions. Paul Dickenson said that perhaps it had been a

Paralympics too far for me. I could deal with that because they were just doing their job. They weren't being malicious or unkind. Afterwards the interviewer gave me a hug and told me to take care of myself.

I didn't know what to do with myself. I was trying to make my way to where my friends were sitting, and on the way several members of the public came up and gave me a hug and told me not to worry. One guy stopped me. He had obviously never competed in an 800 metres in his life. He was overweight, and I remember him telling me that I had chosen the wrong tactics! He was right, but I didn't need to be told that. It was hard not to be rude. I just wanted to get to my friends and my daughter and be with them.

I finally got to the stands. My close friend Maureen and her husband Ray and their daughter Sarah (they were looking after my daughter Carys while I was at the Games), were obviously upset. Two of my oldest friends were are also there, Ric and his wife Julie, and their three daughters, who are my god-daughters. They didn't seem to know what to say.

The only person who wasn't upset was Carys. She was walking around, seemingly oblivious to everything, and I turned to her and said, 'Did you see Mummy's race?' She looked me straight back in the eye, and replied, 'No, I was eating a hot dog.'

This immediately broke the tension. I remember my friends joining in the laughter. It made me realize that, while athletics was incredibly important to me and my family, and the people who care about me or the sport, at the end of the day, it was just one race. It was a big race to lose, but just one race in my career.

Later that night, with Jenni, team coach Jason and Ian, we tried to figure out what had gone wrong. The fact was that it could have been anything. It could have been my attitude going into the race, and me thinking that I couldn't win. It could have been my indecision, or it could just have been that there were six better people than me in the race. You can analyse things too much, and sometimes there is no answer.

But training during the next two days was one of the hardest things I've ever done. I needed to get some confidence back, and I needed to do everything I could to go out and win, to prove to myself that it wasn't a Paralympics too far, and that I wasn't past my best. I had had a good season. I had won a lot of races, and I knew that my form couldn't possibly have completely deserted me overnight.

I had the option of going home. I had been told that I didn't need to compete. But I knew that I wanted to stay and see what happened. Part of this desire was to confront my worse fear (losing) and just be there.

Jenni came out and trained with me. She was going through a really tough time at the Games. Things had not worked out for her, but still she came to the track to help me.

Leaving the track and going back to the village was always a bit scary because there were guard dogs on duty – and that night we were chased. I remember laughing, almost hysterically, that my Paralympic career could be ended, not by my being rubbish, but by two really ugly dogs.

On the day of my 100 metres final, I was perhaps the most nervous I had ever been in my life. Normally it is quite usual for me to be sick during the warm-up. Nerves affect everyone in different ways. Before this particular race I was sick twelve times. Jason was allocated as coach to look after me and he stayed by my side, getting me drinks and ice, and just talking to me. Ian was there, working with a number of other athletes. I didn't want to disappoint him any more than I felt I had already done.

As I was leaving the warm-up track, Ian came over to me and smiled, and said good luck. Jason looked at me and told me I was the best in the world, and that I could win. Those two small things were amazingly comforting to me.

But, even more touching, one of my main competitors – Francesca Porcellato from Italy – came up and asked me if I was OK. We have known each other a long time, and have competed against each other since 1990. I looked at her and told her that after the 800 metres I was feeling pretty bad. Francesca had won a medal in the race.

She looked at me and smiled. She told me that I was the best in the world, and that over the 100 metres that season no one had come near me, and that it was my race to win. What was amazing was that in every 100 metres race we had competed in that year, she had come second. She had the most to win, if I lost. It would be her chance to win gold. She could have said something that would have messed up my head, and made me lose concentration before the race. But she didn't.

Francesca's actions and words were one of the kindest things that anyone has ever done for me in sport.

Going out on to the track for the final, I was sick one more time as we waited. The wait seemed to go on forever. As we lined up on the start line, I remember my hands shaking and I could barely keep them still as the starter called us to the line. I just thought about what Francesca had said.

I had drawn a middle lane, with Francesca on my left, and an American on my right. The US girl had a good start, but Francesca had a blinder. However, although she got out of the blocks so incredibly quickly, for once I didn't panic. I knew that if I could get past her I would be OK.

By 60 metres I was alongside her.

Then I relaxed, and I won the race.

I was the happiest I had ever been after a race. Leaving the track this time I felt great. The BBC did a more positive interview this time, and Ian looked relieved. I joined my friends on the stands, and they were so pleased it was a delight to be with them.

Only Carys was looking a little grumpy. When, once again, I asked if she had seen my race, she glowered at me. She told me that she had been told by Maureen that she wasn't allowed to have an ice-cream unless she watched me race. And she told me that she had. Once again, her attitude lightened the situation.

The next race, the 400 metres, was my only event that wasn't held in the evening. I had qualifying rounds for the 200 metres the evening before and knew that I wasn't going to get much sleep. I pushed well in the 200 metres rounds, and got through to the final, but had to rush back to the village to eat, and rest.

To race at nine o'clock in the morning meant that I had to be up at around four thirty. Ian was less than happy to be up at that time, but he got up to be with me for the race.

Going on to the track I looked across to the finish line and saw the BBC presenters Clare Balding and Colin Jackson. Both just looked at me and nodded.

The semi-final had been close. I had drawn a good semi and had won. The second semi, which I managed to watch track-side, had been won by Madeline Nordlund from Sweden in a new Paralympic record. Francesca Porcellato had been second.

For the final I had the best chance that I could have. Madeline was not a quick starter, but a fast finisher. Francesca was on my outside and was a quick starter and – once she hit her top speed – was very consistent, but she didn't really have a big kick. I knew that I had to start fast, to try to make Madeline panic, and then not give her enough room to pull me in.

Francesca went off very quickly, and my plan was to work on the first 200 metres, to be past her by the half way point, and then just bury myself until the finish line.

I only remember the first 50 metres. I got on to Francesca's shoulder at the 50 metres mark and by the 100 metres mark I knew that I was past her. I don't remember much else about the race. With 20 metres to go I could feel Madeline coming up behind me, and my only thoughts were about keeping my technique right, and finishing.

I didn't have the energy to do a lap of honour, and in any case the crowds were quiet, because it was early on a Sunday morning. Going over to be interviewed, I was asked by Clare how it felt to be Britain's most successful

Paralympian. For once, I couldn't think of too much to say. I muttered something about it being great, and then I probably gave the cheesiest answer that I have ever given. I said that I was glad that I hadn't got the film crew out of bed so early for nothing…

But winning that medal meant a lot to me because, as Clare said, I was now Britain's most successful Paralympian. It's a strange title to have, and it's a title I will probably only hold for one four-year cycle, as there are a couple of swimmers who are on high medal targets and have a couple more Games in them.

But it is something very nice to hold on to for a while. There is a difference between a gold medal and a record, whether British or world. No one can ever take my medal away from me. It doesn't matter whether it was a good or bad race. World records are wonderful to hold, but they are transitory. At some point, sooner or later, someone will take them away. So you just enjoy them for a while.

Leaving Athens was an emotional experience. I had been through so much in two short weeks, and so had my family. I longed to be back in my own house, back training, and back to normality.

The most important lesson I learnt from this experience was who my true friends in sport were. They were the people who didn't tell me what to do, but questioned some of the decisions I was taking. They asked me to think about whether I now wanted to retire, and were honest about what they thought I could still achieve in sport. Some thought I should stop, others that I should carry on, but the real friends let me make the decision for myself.

Those friends have stayed with me throughout the rest of my career. And I have made new ones along the way who offer me the same sensitive advice and support. These are the people whom I trust with the rest of my career.

CHAPTER FIVE

Making It Happen!

People are always interested in the details of my life and how I train. Like all athletes I have to look after myself and eat sensibly. On a typical day I'll have toast or porridge for breakfast, with coffee; a sandwich and fruit for lunch, and pasta or rice in the evening. I'm not the best cook in the world!

My weakness is probably drinking too much coffee – my favourite is single shot grande caramel latte, from Starbucks. Ian laughs at me a lot because this is one thing that I am really fussy about.

I train six days a week so I need plenty of sleep and try to get to bed reasonably early.

People prepare and train in different ways but there are a few fixed realities in sport, which are the same for everyone.

First, you have a very limited time in which to achieve. You have to be gaining qualifying marks in your late teens or early twenties to be able to qualify for the national teams and then make it to major Games. You cannot go back. In many professions you can take a career break, or go back and re-sit exams, but you can't go back to a Paralympics.

It is often said that one of the most important things an athlete can have is parents who can pass the right genes on to you. What is certainly true is that the time of year you are born can make a difference. At seventeen, for some sports, you can fail to make it to major Games, simply because you haven't matured enough physically, mentally or emotionally. Six months either side can make a huge difference. The dates of the Olympics and Paralympics are set in stone. The same is true for World Championships, Commonwealth Games, and national and regional championships. They all play their part in the developmental ladder that athletes have to work through in order to compete at the 'big' ones. Some athletes jump a couple of steps, but most work from the bottom up, and the timing of those, in relation to an athlete's age, can be crucial.

Athletes don't have the power to change any of this, nor the date or timing of their events during the Games. You just have to fit in with what is there.

If you are aiming to win a gold medal at a major Games event (which is what team mates and sponsors want from you) then that is when you have to deliver. Not a week before or a week after. You can win every event in a championship season but the general public, sports administrators and the media will only remember who won the big one.

Second, no athlete has a right to win a medal. Athletes can go into major Games as favourite or underdog. But apart from the psychological benefits or disadvantages this might bring, on the day it is a split second of time that will decide who wins and who doesn't. In Britain we love the underdog, the people who come from behind, or who deal well with adversity. That is what made Eddie the Eagle so popular. But for those who want – and need – to win, there is only one way to increase your chances of doing so, and that is to train.

There are many things that I have learnt through competing in sport – and you have to keep learning if you want to be the best. Sport is about much more than physical training. I have learnt how to manage my time, plan my life, and also find out some of the ways that I can, and can't, achieve.

51

'Individual' sports are not necessarily about individuals. For some reason that I have never quite understood, people often want to split sport into two categories: 'individual' and 'team' sports. Competitors are seen as belonging to either one or the other. People talk about the differences in personality or character that are required for each.

I have been asked numerous times throughout my career whether I am a 'team player', the assumption being that because I compete as an individual, I can't be. But in truth there is very little that I do on my own. The only time that I am ever truly alone is when I am on the track competing.

Wheelchair racing is seen an individual sport as opposed to a team sport. But in both kinds of sports you need a strong character and personality, and the ability to deal with adversity and success.

Whichever path a competitor chooses to follow, you need similar qualities, and, if you don't already have them, you need to develop them. Personally, I find that having good relationships with the people I work with is crucial. Very few of us can get through life entirely on our own. You may not choose to be friends with the people that you work with, and you may not hang out together after work, but you need to know their strengths and weaknesses, and respect both, and be able to work with them.

For most of my time in sport, I have had a (varying) group of people around me to help me achieve my goals. Though most of my training sessions are spent on my own, these people advise me, and help me work on my training plans and fitness so that I am the best that I can be.

In this team are people I trust implicitly because I know they not only care about me as an athlete, but they care about me as a person, on and off the track. I don't always do everything they think I should do, but their advice is always valuable. They provide me with a fresh perspective on what I am trying to achieve, and the way that I am trying to achieve it.

The group around me includes my family and friends, coaches, training partners, physiotherapists, masseurs, sports scientists, dieticians and sports psychologists. I joke that I don't yet have a psychiatrist, but I am always open to offers!

My family are, of course, very much a part of this. They have always been there for me, encouraging me to try new things, and be the best that I can be. I don't remember a time when they explicitly said this, but the support was always there. Even now they will give me very honest answers to anything I ask: about the quality of the race I have just done, about my answers in an interview, or on the colour of the suit that I was wearing! That is what families are for – and if your family can't tell you things like that, then who can? I don't always react well to all their advice, but I try to accept it in the spirit it is given. Perhaps we should all spend more time thinking about how we interact with people. It is easy to get annoyed when someone tells you something that you don't want to hear, but in fact how you react is important to your development. I think that we are conditioned not to like people who don't agree with the things that we believe in, or have an opposing view. I know that in the past this has been true of me. However, I know that my family, and the people around me that I trust, give criticism with the best of intentions.

Planning is essential to make things happen. It isn't enough simply to know what you want to do. I learnt from my father than unless you understand your sport, and plan for it, you are just wandering around in the dark. I learnt to talk to other athletes about how the structure of the sport worked. I spoke to local and national coaches to understand the system. I sometimes talk about athletics being a 'game', but that is to put down the sport I love. It is vital that all athletes properly understand their sports. It is not enough simply to train in a vacuum, even if you are training to your maximum capability. To have any chance of fulfilling your ultimate wish – being selected for the team – to happen, you have to know the qualifying dates for selection, the method of selection, even who is going to be on the panel and how they want the information they require to be presented to them.

It comes back to that crucial rule: you have to be on the start line as an absolute minimum if you want a chance of winning a race. You can be the fastest person in the world, but unless you fulfil the selection criteria, you won't be there. And winning a string of races won't matter, unless you win the major champi-onships. As I was told many years ago by a coach, no one remembers who comes second, and it doesn't matter what you win before or after, it is the big events that count.

Finding out how it all worked made me realise that most of my success would be down to me. What I did every single day in training would impact on what I could achieve. Unless I trained hard, unless I tried to live as an athlete, I wouldn't get into a position to be selected.

But, of course, you need to know what to train at. And the hard part of planning is learning what is best to do, and acting on it, so you can make your dream happen.

Sometimes, if an athlete has a poor race, it is possible to blame other people. You say 'she blocked me in', 'she pushed me out', 'those two girls worked together against me'. Or 'my chair wasn't set up right' or 'my gloves didn't work'. Sometimes, indeed, these things happen. I was at a race last summer when the glove of one of the athletes fell apart. He stopped, grabbed another athlete who had finished racing, and took one of his. An athlete I coach, Brian Alldis, while in a short sprint, lost his glove about 40 metres from the line. It flew off in an arc, nearly hitting several other athletes. I know plenty of competitors who would have just coasted the last 40 metres to the finish line. It was only one race – what would it matter in the scheme of things? But of course it could matter. What if that race had been the last opportunity for the athlete to qualify for the Paralympics? What if it had been the qualifying round for the Paralympic final, and the athlete was in the position to make it through?

The athlete must react instantly. There is no time to think about what to do. This athlete knew he had to get to the finish line. He carried on pushing, probably adding minor scratches to his hands. If he hadn't carried on he might not have made the start line in future competitions. In fact the race was a high level international, and if he hadn't finished it wouldn't have counted against him. The event wasn't his strongest distance, he had already qualified for the World Championships, and he had other events that week where he could prove his fitness.

But for me it was important that he carried on and finished. Afterwards he went and retrieved his glove, and made sure it was OK. And, crucially, he learnt a lesson. He learnt that if the same was ever to happen in a bigger race – his Paralympic final, say – it wouldn't be the end of the world. He could carry on and he could finish. And that is what being an athlete is all about.

Equipment can fail, of course, but when you are planning and training you work to minimise the risks. We don't often travel with a mechanic in tow and over the years I have learned to fix things myself. I always check my equipment is all there, and working correctly, and try to cover all the bases.

Worrying is sometimes seen as a negative emotion, but it does help you prepare for things that might happen. Worrying is what pushes you to anticipate what might go wrong, and plan accordingly.

It is important to train as hard as you are going to race. You cannot train at one level and then expect to step up to a higher level in a competition. Any athlete can have a blast of a day and perform way above the level that they are expected to, but this doesn't guarantee long term success.

Consistency in training and racing is also very important, but there is a difference between having a sensible routine and using irrational routine as a crutch to lean on. I knew an athlete who, before a race, always *had* to eat a certain sort of food. I knew another who was convinced that he couldn't perform unless he listened to a certain piece of music before he went on to the track. The day that he got to the track and the batteries died in his CD player was a disaster. He had nobody to run around and find batteries for him and he was too stressed-out to do it himself. He didn't get to hear his music and he fell apart.

I have never believed in using such routines, because I know how bad I am at temporarily losing things! I do have a routine that I use for warming up, but it's adaptable. Sometimes we don't have a track to warm up on which is separate from the competing track, so you have to be flexible.

On the other hand, I do mind who I share rooms with when I travel, and I have never felt guilty about this. When you have spent perhaps two years training specifically for an event, the choice of person who is with you for the final moments is important. At something like a Paralympic Games, you are away from all the normal things in your life. Family have limited access, you may be sharing an apartment with seven other people, some of whom you don't know very well, and the food may be exotic or just bad and not what you are used to. The last thing you want is to have to spend lots of time in a room with a person you don't get on with. Having said that, sometimes you do have to share with a person you don't know very well, and then you just have to make the best of it, and not let little things upset you.

Since I started competing I have kept a training diary. When times are tough it is useful to be able to look back and see what I have done. To the younger athletes that I coach, I also suggest that they shouldn't only keep a training diary, but also a diary of the people that they race against. I ask them to keep notes (however short) on the way that they perform. It is amazing how many athletes will race the same way, and it helps to learn their patterns for when they meet up competitively again.

CHAPTER SIX

What I've Learned Along The Way

I meet lots of young people every year, both with and without impairments. I remember when I was a teenager being asked by adults what I wanted to do when I grew up; now I am one of those adults, and ask the same thing.

It amazes me how many young people just look and shrug and say 'I don't know'. And it scares me when young people who do know what they want to do have no clue, or have taken no action, to enable them to achieve it.

I met a young girl about two years ago who, when I asked her what she wanted to be, looked at me and said 'a pop star'. I asked her if she was in a band. She said no. I asked if she played a musical instrument. Again she said no. When I asked if she was in a choir, sang with her family, or did anything musical at all, she said no each time. When I asked her how she was going to achieve her ambition, she smiled broadly and said, 'I'm going to win *Pop Idol*.' It is sometimes hard not to despair that so many feel that the way to achieve anything is through the media, or by taking short cuts. Of course miracles can happen, but even when they do, most people find that they have to work extremely hard afterwards.

There was a tiny part of me that smiled at her ambition (because it is important to have a dream) but mostly I was sad, because the chances of her achieving her ambition, without doing anything herself to increase that chance, were so remote.

When you see media reports about stars being 'discovered' overnight, you only have to delve a little beneath the surface to reveal the hard work that has been involved. Years of acting classes, performing schools and competitions, make the 'overnight discovery' tag amusing. It simply makes a better story for the media, if they can claim a Cinderella moment. And it feeds that small part of everyone which hopes that we will have our lives changed or fulfilled by a chance discovery, or that we will one day win the lottery and our lives will be changed for ever...

You need to have a goal, or dream. You need to be able to plan how to get there. (Or get someone else to do it effectively – this is why so many athletes have coaches who help them deliver their goals.)

You need discipline that enables you to go out and do not just the nice, easy things, but also the things that are a challenge.

You need self-belief. Although this may be challenged from time to time, really successful people are those who are able to deal with failure. Anyone can be successful once, but coming back from failure is a huge challenge, and one that not everyone wants to do, or can do. It means building on the hard days, when times are tough, and coming out the other side. You also of course have to learn to deal with success and not get carried away by it, believing that you are invincible.

You need to develop good relationships – and having a group of people you can trust around you is very important. These may be people who don't have exactly the same goals as you, but they can still help you on your way.

You need to take time to balance your professional goals with your family and friends and the people that you care about.

And you need to treat the people around you with respect – the way that you yourself would like to be treated. It is truer in sport than in any other field that you meet the same people on the way up as you meet on the way down. Early on, while you are developing, arrogance can be a big strength, but humility is good to have too.

There are four aspects to achievement. You have to know what you want to achieve, where you are now, how you plan to get where you want to go, and what work you need to do to get there.

You should begin with the end in mind – and work back from there. Don't start by just knowing where you are now, and assume you will get to your goal somehow. You need to write a plan of all the steps that are needed along the way, and you need to anticipate the ups and downs you might encounter. Without a plan, while you might indeed move in a certain direction, you could find out that this is the wrong direction.

You may feel that there are lots of things that you want to achieve. I have many goals for my sport, and many goals for my personal life too. What is vital is working out which are the important ones, and which the realistic ones, and how they affect each other.

Some goals may appear to be more urgent

than others, simply because there are time lines associated with them. Or they may be goals that other people want you to achieve. It really helps if you write those goals down and think about how they fit into your larger plan, so you can prioritise what you want to do. You may not be able to achieve everything that you want – so make sure you pick the right goals!

Some time-management organisers say that writing lists is not constructive, because it doesn't help you prioritise. But I like writing lists, and I often use post-it notes, because I can move them around. Once I have my collection of notes, and have put them roughly into the order that I want to do things, then I can move on to the next step. As you write the plan you may find that the order changes, but this is all part of the process of working through the steps.

Once you have listed your goals, you have to ask yourself: where am I now? To be able to plan anything, you have to know where the starting point is. You wouldn't decide to go on a family day out to the local park with no clue as to where it was. You wouldn't take your family out to wander around randomly until you happened to find it.

Planning to be an athlete (or other achiever) you need the same fore-knowledge. You need to know your starting point, and there are many ways to achieve this. You may talk to your coach (or boss), or your friends, you may look at your personal (all-time) and season-best performances. You could also look at how you competed against other people, scoring points for victories and taking them away for losses.

However, this can only give you a small part of the overall picture. Some of the information will be subjective. The objective stuff can be harder to obtain.

You have to know what you are good at, and not so good at, and where you could improve. But that can be tough. If you ask your boss, say, he might not want to tell you about things that you are bad at, because you might get upset, and that would bring a different set of problems to deal with. Your friends and family, on the other hand, may be a little too open. Because of their closeness to you, and because you asked the question, they may feel that they can let rip with everything critical they feel about you.

The answer is to lay ground rules. You should explain what you are hoping to get from them, and that you are looking for responses that that will affect you positively, rather than make you defensive. (If all you want to hear is that you are brilliant, then only ask your mum. But if you want to hear what you can do to improve yourself, you must ask other people.)

Give them a list of key areas that you would like to talk about, and govern the time that you spend with them. You don't want to turn it into a three hour meeting from which, at the end, you get nothing.

Something that we have used from time to time is a SWAT analysis, which anyone can do. You look at your strengths, weaknesses, opportunities and threats, and name your goals. Then, at a carefully guided meeting, outlining what you can and cannot say, we share that information with other people. This can be done with several people at a time, in the context of what everyone is trying to achieve.

Once you know what you want to achieve, and you have got other people's input on it, you are really in a position to work out where you are now. From this you can work out honestly what skills you already have, and which you need to work on.

If you know accurately where you are, you can measure improvement. You now know your start and end point, and can sit down and plan the steps that you need to take. This can be a detailed list, or a time line, or any way that works well for you. I write my winter training programme in quite general terms first, looking at what I need to achieve each month, and then I fill in the details below that. So by the start of winter training I know pretty much all the sessions that I need to do for the following year. This may change, when I either reach or don't reach my targets (sometimes illness can get in the way or you can progress quicker than expected). But it is easier to change a plan than try to write it as you go along.

Once you have completed the first two steps of planning – knowing your goals, and where exactly you are starting from – you have to write down your plan. This is the step that may take the longest, and for many is the least interesting. It will be a personal training plan, as in the business world it would be a personal development plan. Whatever format the plan takes, you need to be able to mark your progress against it to see that things are moving in the right direction. It is better to find out three months ahead of major Games that some things haven't worked in training, rather than finding out the night before an event.

Then, the fourth step: you have to follow your plan. Anyone can train hard, and some people find it easy, but others find this the biggest challenge. I have met many athletes who are talented, but who lack the ability to push themselves really hard in training.

Often the things that you are not so good at are the things you least like doing, and you are tempted to ignore them. At work, people will often ignore things in their inbox in favour of tasks that seem more appealing, or that will take less time. Anything that is challenging seems difficult. This is why planning ahead is important, so that you can be sure you have put aside time specifically to complete these tasks.

The world of athletics is not unique – it is about building on success in the same way as you build a house with bricks. You have to get the foundations right, and then you can practise and improve and reach your peak.

Even when you know yourself, and have your plan, you will, as an athlete, have to make some tough decisions. Are you going to work on the things that you are weakest at, where you can possibly make a big improvement, or is it best to work on the things that you are better at, to make the most of your natural talents? For me, my top speed is one of my huge strengths. I can push very fast over short to medium distances. What I am not good at is starting. Some years I work more on my starts than on my top speed, but the pattern can change. Coming up to major Games I may be working on both things at the same time. What is important is that whatever decision you make, it must be an informed one. In wheelchair racing, for instance, it is highly unlikely that if you never practise a start you will ever be really good at them!

Once you reach your peak you should 'tell the world' about your goals. This is definitely one of the things that has contributed to my success If you have a dream and share it with others, it puts pressure on you to try and achieve. It also makes that dream more real. While dreams remain in your head, they may never progress; but vocalising them brings them alive and moves them forward. Just writing the dreams down doesn't do the job. You have to vocalise. It is about making things happen.

Before the Games at Athens I spent six

months doing interviews with journalists, and everyone one of them asked me what medals I was going to win. The scenario I came up with was two golds, one silver and a bronze. My own personal goal was a little higher, but what I told the journalists was what I thought I could realistically achieve. And from the moment I told the first journalist that this was what I wanted to do, the motivation to train was there for every session that I did.

I often get asked for advice by young athletes, and I'm happy to try to answer questions. But some of the training sessions that I do are not appropriate for someone who is just developing in the sport. And few problems in sport, such as how to acquire the technique for pushing a chair, have a ten-minute quick-fix solution. Yes, in ten minutes I can show someone what they should be aiming for, but to perfect that technique the athlete will have to do it again and again in training to embed it into their brain. It may seem tempting to blame equipment and try to solve difficulties with a new chair, or a new pair of gloves, but the solving of most athletes' problems only comes from learning a good technique, and then training hard.

Over the years I have seen many naturally talented athletes who possessed the potential to go far, but what has stopped them from achieving this potential was their inability to learn, or train hard.

Gary Player is reputed to have said, 'the harder I train the luckier I become'. Practice can indeed make perfect. A reality of life is that some people are more naturally talented than others. Some people make everything they do look easy. Some people are natural risk-takers, while others are reluctant to try anything new. We can change some of the ways in which we behave, but we can't completely change our personality.

An American athlete, Jim Knaub, who had eight Boston Wheelchair Marathon victories behind him, once said, 'It isn't always the fastest person who wins, it is the person who slows down the least'.

When I was growing up, I wasn't the most talented, but I was keen. I knew many very talented young boys and girls in school who were competing at a good level. In fact they had a great deal more natural talent than me. But at the highest level in any walk of life, natural talent is not enough. Training made the difference to what I was able to do. When natural talent runs out, what else do you have to fall back on? You need the ability to push yourself as hard as you can, and you need to be able to pick yourself up from disasters. You get the confidence to do this from working to the highest level that you can.

Sport and life are full of ups and downs. There is rarely an easy path open to anyone. Even for those who are seen to be the most successful, there are usually things thrown in their path which would test anyone's resolve.

For me, a big part of my life has been about dealing with what I have got, good or bad, and then trying to move on, to get to a point where I can reach my goals.

I would love to say that there is a solution out there for every problem. There probably isn't, but I do believe that you can work through to get on the path to your end goal if you are committed to the task and work hard.

I have been very fortunate to have had a great time being an athlete. I have had the opportunity to represent my country, work with some amazing coaches, and also achieve many of my goals. But once my sporting life is over then there will always be other goals that replace my desire to break world records and win gold medals.

The life of an athlete is short. You spend more of your life not competing than competing. I have been really lucky, not to have picked up any major injuries, and only had brief periods where I wasn't able to train or compete. But one thing I do know is that the rest of my life will be filled with other challenges that will become equally important to me, and that they will replace what I feel for wheelchair racing.

Working with up-and-coming athletes is a great deal of fun, and if I can help the athletes that I coach to reach their maximum potential (whether this is representing their country, or winning medals, or just them being the best they can), then I will be happy. I have one thing when coaching that I hold dear. I coach athletes whom I like as people. To really want to help them, to sometimes have to be really tough on them, to pick them up when they are down, it is important for me to have that basic level of trust and respect for them as individuals. I hope that I will never coach an athlete who I don't like first and foremost.

Throughout my athletics career I have enjoyed working with and in the media, presenting TV and radio programmes, commentating on sports events and also writing many articles for a wide variety of journals, magazines and newspapers. Right now that work looks set to continue and develop and that is a really exciting challenge ahead for me.

When I know that the time is right to stop, then I will not have any regrets about ending my athletics career. There may have been a couple of races that I could have done differently, but actually I have come to terms with the fact that winning 11 gold Paralympic medals is OK – it was always something that I wanted to do, and I have done it. At Paralympic level I don't think that I could have done any more. My sister summed it up for me in really simple terms. She told me that I only have to prove things to myself. The rest doesn't matter. I have proved to myself that I am a good athlete, and I have competed well.

I have always known that one day I would wake up and just wouldn't want to do wheelchair racing at international level any more. It wouldn't be a slow, protracted decision – it would be quite immediate. I knew after Athens that I wouldn't compete in Beijing (I don't think a lot of people believed me when I said this in just about every interview I have done). When you have been around as long as I have, then many people just presume that you will keep going forever. But Athens wasn't quite the time to stop. There were a couple more things that I wanted to do, and I want to finish my international career in an event that is held on British soil.

I will always want to be fit and healthy. I don't think that I will ever stop training in my chair or on my bike, but I don't always want to be an athlete.

There is one thing that I know. As one door closes another one opens, and there are plenty of challenges and goals that I still have in my life that will keep me Aiming High.